Clarence Powell is one of the Kingdom's ___ ___
agement. God has gifted him with an encouraging tongue and
pen. His use of humor and wisdom connects wonderfully well with
the listener and reader. He continues to touch hearts with the love
and warmth of the Lord Jesus His recent work, Insiders and Out-
siders, is a collection of spiritual gems that will stir the heart with
strength and hope for daily living.

Alan Miller, Minister and Friend

I've enjoyed Clarence Powell's earlier book, Daily Grace, which
comes in bite-sized chunks that can be read as a daily devotional.
The readings often have surprising insights, worthy of pausing to
digest or triggering another line of thinking. Capable of reading
on several levels, most folk will enjoy and benefit from this book
and its continuation in this next volume.

Perry Lassiter
Pastor, Writer, Pastoral Counselor

Clarence Powell is an encourager, a communicator, a gifted sto-
ryteller and a friend. I have been blessed over the years by his in-
sight into human nature and his Godly wisdom. He writes from his
heart - a heart truly touched by God's grace. All who read his work
will be greatly blessed.

Lee McGlone, Senior Pastor
First Baptist Church
Arkadelphia, Arkansas

Insiders

AND
Outsiders

Brief Meditations
On Eternal Truths

Clarence Powell

Cover and Title Page Designs by Julie Cupples

Also by Clarence Powell - Daily Grace: Brief Meditations on Eternal Truths

Dedication

With deepest gratitude for

The residents of the Louisiana Baptist Children's Home
They taught me courage in adversity

The Staff At The Louisiana Baptist Children's Home
I was so blessed to be associated with these
very special servants of the Lord.

The Family
They accepted my concern for other people's children.
They filled our house with laughter and our days with joy.
They have made me so proud. I am so blessed.
*I have no greater joy than to hear that
my children walk in truth.* (3 John 4)

Letha
The love of my life
Burdens were lighter and joys more
abundant because she shared
them. She makes this journey
a joyful celebration.

The Savior
His presence has sustained me.
His sacrificial love still astounds me.

Thanks to my editors, Karan Blankenship & Sara Barefoot.

From the Author

If failures and mistakes have made you feel like an outsider to the family of God until you discovered the joy of God's forgiving and restoring grace, I'm sure we are related and I take joy in calling myself your brother.

Table of Contents

Insiders and Outsiders

Ephesians 2:19
*We are no longer strangers, but fellow citizens
with the saints and members of the household
of God.*

I was spending Sunday afternoon with my friend, Jimmy. That day, his older sister and older brother also had company. Jimmy decided that instead of playing Gene Autry and Roy Rogers we would hang out with the big kids. Their response to this was to tell us to get lost. When they went out behind the chicken house, we followed. So they ran to the tractor shed where we followed again. By then the chase had become a serious matter for Jimmy.

We followed them from the tractor shed to the hay stack and finally to the barn where they went into the cotton seed room and locked the door. When Jimmy asked to be let in, they told him to scram. Then he began to cry and kick on the door, demanding to be let in. When they began to laugh, he began to cry, curse, and kick even harder on the door. Unfortunately there was an ax lying nearby. Now, in uncontrollable anger he attacked the lock with the ax. With each swing of the ax he cried, "Let me in!" Finally, with the lock section of the door in splinters, the door swung open. His brother and sister said, "Mmmh Mmmh look what you done went and done." His response was one he thought surely everyone should understand. He said, "I just wanted to be in here with you."

Over the years I have seen many folks who were crying, sometimes cursing and doing destructive things just because they felt like outsiders and wanted to be insiders.

In our struggle against insignificance, we try so desperately to become insiders hoping that our identification with others will show the world that we really do matter. Then when the loneliness is almost more than one can bear, we hear the amazing news. God loves us and we are called to belong to Him. We really do matter.

 Lord, forgive me for seeking significance in anything other than in the awesome truth that I belong to You.

 Yes, Jesus loves me.
   Yes, Jesus loves me.

Honk If You Love Jesus

Matthew 16:24
Then Jesus said to His disciples, " If anyone desires to come after Me, let him deny himself, and take up his cross, and follow Me.

While waiting at a traffic light, two young women pulled up beside me in a convertible. They were playing very loud heavy metal music, bouncing around in the front seat, and dressed in a manner that made me wonder if their mothers knew they were outside. After the light changed, as they pulled away, I noticed the bumper sticker. It said "Honk If You Love Jesus."

Now, I really didn't know what to do. If I honk at them, will I appear to be another "dirty old man?" If I don't honk, will it appear that I don't love Jesus? As I wrestled with this theological dilemma, I began to wonder if there really was any correlation between my horn and my heart.

Can it be that our present culture would reduce discipleship to a matter of bumper stickers and reduce the sharing of our faith to a matter of honking horns? There have indeed been times when we have sought an easier discipleship and a less costly commitment. After all, bumper stickers are cheap and honking horns requires little effort. However, when Jesus spoke of denying our selves, taking up crosses and following Him to Calvary, He took away the easy options.

Lord, when You chose to declare Your love for me, You never honked a horn on an ox cart. Neither was it with clever slogans or empty gestures, but by being nailed to the cross and giving Your life for me. Returning such love to You is neither easy, cheap nor convenient.

Love so amazing so divine
Demands my life, my soul, my all

Cactus Logic

Galatians 5:22-23
But the fruit of the Spirit is love, joy, peace, patience kindness, goodness, faithfulness, gentleness, self control...

Recently, in a moment of unjustifiable anger over an issue, I spoke harshly and unkindly to someone who deserved better than that from me. Later, when I went to him and asked for his forgiveness, he graciously forgave me and prayed for me. I tried to think of a profound, intelligent explanation. (I was really looking for an excuse for the inexcusable.) The closest I could come was the case of the cowboy who was riding across the prairie. Suddenly, he stopped, got off his horse, took off all his clothes and jumped onto a bed of cactus plants. When he was asked why, he said, "At the time, it just seemed like the thing to do."

If you would pray for me, please ask that I have wisdom enough not to do something permanently stupid when I'm temporarily upset.

Please ask that the Holy Spirit bear an abundance of the fruit of kindness, goodness, gentleness and self control in my life. Maybe I can put the cactus behind me. On second thought, may the Lord remove it.

Lord, please draw me so close to You that my relationship with You may mold and shape my relationships with others.

 I am loved. You are loved.
Won't you please take my hand.
We are free to love each other.
We are loved.

Kingdom Hillbillies

Ephesians 2:19
*Now, therefore, you are no longer strangers
and foreigners, but fellow citizens with the
saints and members of the household of God.*

When Jed Clampett and his kin became fabulously wealthy, they left their one room cabin in the hills and moved into a Beverly Hills mansion. Although their residency changed, there was little change in their life-style. They still rode in an aging rattletrap truck. Jethro was still dumb as a post. Ellie Mae still hung out with her "critters". Granny still made homemade lye soap and cooked possum, hog jowls and gopher stew.

One day, Jesus purchased our salvation and through faith in Him, we became fellow citizens with the saints and members of the household of God. We are now citizens of God's kingdom. Our new citizenship offers us a life of joy and peace. Why should we bring from the backwoods of our past lives those practices and attitudes that deprive us of the highest and best that the Kingdom has to offer? Why should my bitterness and resentment deprive me of loving relationships? Why should the practices of my old life rob me of an intimate relationship with the King Who loves me and has called me to be like Him.

Lord, thank You for inviting me into Your kingdom. Open my eyes to the glory and high privilege that my new citizenship offers me. Forgive me for clinging to that which is unworthy of the kingdom.

 *O what peace we often forfeit
O what needless pain we bear
All because we do not carry
Everything to God in prayer.*

Duck Logic

Proverbs 7:23
He did not now that it would cost him his life.

A duck walked into a bakery and said, "I'll have two pork chops." The manager responded by explaining, "You can't get pork chops in a bakery." The next day and each day for a week, the duck came in asking for two pork chops only to be told that you can't get pork chops in a bakery. Finally, the manager said, "If you come in here and ask for pork chops again, I'm going to nail your feet to the floor."

The next day the duck came in and asked, "Do you have any nails?" The manager said, "Of course we don't have any nails, this is a bakery." So the duck said, "Then I'll have two pork chops."

It's always wise to consider consequences before making choices. Some choices are more costly than others. Some choices are more dangerous than others.

To choose to follow Christ is indeed costly. It will cost you your old life style. It will cost you your right to maintain total control of your own life. Still, to reject Him will prove to be even more costly.

The Savior's love for you, His promise to walk with you and His promise to take you home with Him to live with Him forever still makes it the safest and wisest choice.

You can't get pork chops in a bakery, but you will feast with the King forever.

Lord, You knew the painful consequences of choosing me but still You chose me and carried the cross to Calvary to pay for my sin and purchase me. Thank You for choosing me. Forgive my foolish choices of the past and lead me to make choices that reflect my devotion to You.

I have decided to follow Jesus.
No turning back. No turning back.

Flea Pickin' Time In Texas

Mark 5:7
I implore You by God that You do not torment me.

Since it has been more than seventy years since the last incident, I suppose it is time for my brothers and me to forgive our sister, Dorothy for the pain she caused us. Back in the late 1930's and early 1940's, in addition to glorious sunrises and breathtaking sunsets, West Texas also had fleas. Dorothy saw fleas, not as pests to be endured, but as enemies to be pursued and attacked with a vengeance. She could spot a flea from across the room and when she did, the near riot would begin. Although we fled in terror, she would chase us until she caught us. Then, she would throw us down onto the ground and begin "the surgical procedure." What she may have lacked in gentleness, she made up for in amazing strength and fierce determination. While we begged, kicked and cried, she pinched, scratched and gouged until she won her victory by removing the flea and a sizable portion of our skin. She didn't seem to mind our cries of pain. All that seemed to matter was conquering the flea.

I can't really blame her for what she did. After all, who wants to sit at the table with flea infested brothers? However, we wished there could have been a kinder, gentler approach. Too often, when a friend has had a flea-sized mote in his eye, my refusal to remove the beam from my own has not allowed me to see his pain or to seek a kinder, gentler approach.

I can't write anymore about gentleness right now because I think my neighbor has a flea.

 Lord, thank You for bearing my grief and carrying my sorrows. Thank You for Your gentle response to my trouble.

 In loving kindness, Jesus came
My soul in mercy to reclaim.

Bulls and Bears

2 Samuel 10:9
When Joab saw that the battle line was against him before and behind...

Cowboy John was being chased by a bull. Around and around the pasture the bull pursued him. John saw a deep hole and jumped into it and the bull rushed by. John immediately climbed out of the hole, only to be chased again. Once more he jumped into the hole. A friend called, "John, stay in the hole!" John cried out, "there's a bear in this hole!"

Often, seeking to solve one problem only exacerbates another one. The choice is not always between safety and danger, but often, between one danger and another. Our difficulty is not usually a single problem. Instead there are multiple problems that complicate each other. I could pay the rent, but there would be no money for groceries. I could purchase groceries, but there would be no money for the rent.

Loneliness is painful, but harmful relationships are likely to cause even more pain. In my loneliness, I long to have something in common with someone else, but participating in their destructive practices is not a good solution.

The good news that we are invited to submit to Him all of life as it is with its abundance of problems and difficulties. We are told that you can *cast all your care on Him for He cares for you.*

Lord, when life is more than I can face or handle, thank You for reaching out Your gentle hand to lift me up and hold me. I place those matters that I cannot handle in Your gentle hands.

I must tell Jesus all of my troubles. I cannot bear these burdens alone; In my distress He kindly will help me; He ever loves and cares for His own.

Fred's Bait Stand

John 6:68
But Simon Peter answered Him, "Lord, to whom shall we go? You have the words of eternal life."

There's an old country song entitled, *"Looking For Love In All The Wrong Places".*

A wife asked her husband to go to the store for bread. He returned later and explained that he could not find any bread at Fred's Bait Stand. The next day she asked him to go to the store for milk. Later he returned explaining the Radio Shack did not have any milk.

Fred is a nice guy and Radio Shack has some interesting stuff, but there are some needs they cannot meet.

When I face uncertainty, I need the One Who invited Me to follow Him. When life is stormy and chaotic, I need the One Who calmed the sea by commanding the winds and the waves to be still. When I am weary of a life that seems to be drying up, I need the Shepherd Who leads me by still waters and invites me to lie down in green pastures.

I still like Fred and I am still intrigued by the gadgets at Radio Shack, but for the hunger of my soul, I need the Savior Who called Himself the Bread Of Life.

Lord, You know all my needs. Forgive me for seeking to meet them in all the wrong places.

 I need Thee, O I need Thee
Every hour I need Thee
O bless me now, my Savior
I come to Thee

The Fence

Hebrews 4:31-32
Let all bitterness, wrath, anger, clamor, and evil speaking be put away from you, with all malice. And be kind to one another, tenderhearted, forgiving one another, even as God in Christ forgave you.

Recently, my brother, Frank, reminded me of an incident that occurred in 1943. When our older brother, A.C. put a single strand electric fence around his pasture, in setting the voltage, he relied on the old maxim that "if a little does a little good..."

One day, a man came out to look at his cattle and was half way over the fence, when he took hold of the wire to push it down and the strong voltage was so painful, he let go and the highly charged wire sprang up between his legs.

Papa was not at all pleased with us for our uproarious laughter, but we had never before seen a grown man dance while straddling an electric fence.

All too often, a small problem is exchanged for a greater one simply because we have been reluctant to take hold of it and handle it while it was small.

The answer to a minor disagreement is not hostility. Unwholesome relationships are not the answer to our loneliness. Resentment and bitterness are not the answer to being offended.

Some things are hard for us to put away on our own. That's why scripture teaches us to *"let them be put away"* by the One Who bore all our grief and carried our sorrows and cried out from the cross, *"Father forgive them..."*

Lord, teach me to know the peace and contentment that comes with a forgiving spirit. Remind me that You have forgiven me of so much more than You have asked me to forgive others.

Join a song with sweet accord and thus surround the throne.

A Convenient Theology

2 Timothy 3:16-17
All Scripture is given by inspiration of God, and is profitable for doctrine, for reproof, for correction, for instruction in righteousness, that the man of God may be complete, thoroughly equipped for every good work.

I guess my interest in theology could be traced to my friend, Vernon. One Sunday afternoon while he was visiting our house, we had some disagreements about what we would do. Each time, Vernon would say, "Clarence, the Bible says you are supposed to do what your company wants to do." So, not willing to risk the wrath of God by disobeying scripture, I yielded. That happened several times that afternoon and I found that following scripture could be rather trying.

A few weeks later I was at his house. When a disagreement arose, I figured that this *"the Bible says"* thing might be a pretty good idea, so I reminded him that the Bible says you must do what your company wants to do. Then, like a patient instructor with a slow learner, Vernon said, "Clarence, the Bible says you don't have to do what your company wants to do all the time."

I suppose this is alright for nine year old boys, but it becomes a sad matter when we quickly use *"the Bible says"* only as a means of getting our own way or putting someone in their place.

The Word of God was not given to us in order that we may be able to lord it over others, but that we may know the love the Savior has bestowed on us and share it with them.

 Lord, give me a greater reverence for Your Word that I may know You better and love You more

 Holy Bible, Book divine,
Precious treasure, thou art mine.

Blind Guides

Matthew 15:14
Let them alone and disregard them; they are blind guides and teachers. And if a blind man leads a blind man, both will fall into a ditch. (AMP)

John, a blind man, asked a stranger on the street how he could find the guide store because he needed to go to the other side of the mountain. He knew the trail was steep and dangerous. He knew that on the trail there were treacherous curves, a snake and a deep pit. The stranger said, "How about that! I'm blind too. I'll be your guide. Since we are both blind, we have so much in common. Along the way, we can commiserate with each other about our blindness and tell of our adventures in our sightless worlds."

John then asked the stranger about the steep curves. The stranger replied, "We will run real fast around them maybe we will not fall over the edge."

John then asked about the snake. The stranger replied, "we'll just get a stick and kill it. And don't worry about the ditch. If we run real fast, maybe we can jump over it."

Later, two snake-bitten blind men were found at the bottom of the ditch.

Without question, we need leadership. Too often we have wanted a leader that is just like us rather than the One Who knows the way, understands the dangers and will keep us from harm.

 Lord, forgive us for listening to the voices of those who are not worthy to be our leaders. Please lead us in paths of righteousness for Your name's sake.

 Savior like a Shepherd lead us.
Much we need Thy tender care.

Fly Drives and Perfect Timing

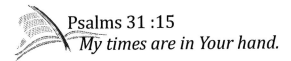 Psalms 31 :15
My times are in Your hand.

In the early 1940's, air conditioning was non-existent for the rural homes of Martin County Texas. In a large family, the screen doors were constantly being opened and sometimes left open. With this situation, flies became a problem. Before each meal, no one sat down until after "the fly drive." All the older members of the family would gather at the back end of our very long kitchen. Each would take a dish towel in each hand and begin waving the towels, driving the flies to the front door.

Often, I had the unenviable task of being the door holder. That may seem like a simple task, but timing was crucial. When the flies were being driven to the door, if the holder waited too long, the flies would circle back to the other end of the kitchen. If the door was opened too soon, the outside flies would get back in. Drivers with the towels were not lacking in advice. Half of them would be yelling, "Hurry up, open it now!" The other half would be yelling, "Not yet! Not yet!" After a failed drive, many none too complimentary remarks were made about the intelligence or the sanity of the door holder.

With my evident lack of timing skills, it's good that I was not the Creator. Imagine catfish, and sharks flopping around on the ground because I had not yet made the lakes and rivers. Imagine elephants, giraffes, hippos and rhinos floating around in space because I had not yet put the dry land in place.

Since I am bombarded with demands to hurry and to slow down, to take quick action and to wait, it's good to place all matters into the hands of the One Whose timing is always right.

 Lord, I stand between my impatience and my reluctance to act. It's Your time.

 In His time. In His time.
He makes all things beautiful in His time.

The Goat Escape

1 John 1:9
If we confess our sins, He is faithful and just to forgive us our sins and to cleanse us from all unrighteousness.

In today's polite society, my uncle Joe would be called an alcoholic. More sophisticated folks may say he "had a dependency." Gentler people may say that "he had issues."

However, in 1940, the less sophisticated and plain spoken folks in Texas referred to him as a drunkard.

My aunt Augusta remained with him because years before she had taken a vow that said, "for better or for worse."

On one occasion when he had been arrested and was facing some serious jail time, Aunt Augusta walked into the Van Zandt County courthouse leading a goat. When the sheriff saw her he swore a little and asked what was going on. Aunt Augusta handed him the rope and said, "Joe has a condition and must have goat's milk three times a day." Then the sheriff resumed his swearing and turned to two deputies and said, "Go get Joe."

Then he handed the rope back to Aunt Augusta and said, "Lady, you take that stinking goat and that stinking low down husband of yours out of here and I don't want to ever see either of you again. Uncle Joe walked away from the jail but he was no different from the man he was before.

I suppose we all have a few goats staked out somewhere: (explanations, excuses and someone else to blame.) However, the excuses, explanations, or other goats are woefully inadequate when the harsh light of truth shines on me and I can no longer pretend that all is well.

I must confess my sin and turn to the One who *"is faithful and just to forgive our sin and to cleanse us from all unrighteousness."*

 Lord, forgive me for all the plans and schemes I use to avoid responsibility for my rebellion and disobedience. I can only turn to You in repentance and thank You for Your forgiving life transforming grace.

 What can wash away my sin?
Nothing but the blood of Jesus.

The Letters

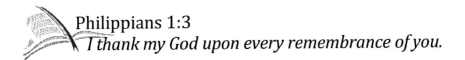

Philippians 1:3
I thank my God upon every remembrance of you.

When a letter arrived from kinfolks, no one opened it but Mama because she was the self appointed official letter reader for the family. We were expected to gather around her while she slowly read the letter emphasizing each word.

All letters followed the same pattern. First there was the greeting, which said, "Dear ones, how are you? We are fine. Hope this finds you the same." Next there would be a remark about the weather. "It sure is hot here" or "We could sure use a good rain." This would be followed with news of illnesses, new babies, or deaths. Then, there would be news of the crops and livestock.

Then, the letter would end abruptly with "Must close, Love Mollie (or Maggie or Minnie or Macie.)

When I was in the army, I was always early for mail call. My standing there in anticipation of mail was not because I wanted a report on Texas crops or weather. I was there because I knew that in each letter, Letha would tell me that she loved me and missed me.

When Paul wrote to his friends in Philippi, there was nothing stale or formal about his letters. He unabashedly shared his deepest feelings.

He could have said, *"It is hot here in Rome. The prison captain has a new horse."* But instead, he said, *"I thank my God on every remembrance of you."*

 Lord, thank You for loving me. Thank for making that love so plain and clear at the cross.

 I love Thee because Thou hast first loved me
And purchased my pardon on Calvary's tree.
I love Thee for wearing the thorns on Thy brow.
If ever I loved Thee, My Jesus tis now.

Cowboy Boots And Bridal Gowns

Psalm 136:1
O Give thanks to the Lord, for He is good, for His steadfast love endures forever. (ESV)

While checking the ads in the "Penny Saver", the local shoppers' newspaper, I was fascinated by two items. The first item said:

> *For Sale: 1 Pair of Cowboy Boots. Size eleven. Never worn. $40.00.*

I wondered who it was that had purchased something as singular as a pair of cowboy boots. Where and with whom had he planned to wear them? Why have they never been worn? Why is he selling them at a fraction of the cost?

The second ad was even more intriguing. It said:

> *For Sale: One beautiful white wedding gown. Size 10. Never Worn. $100.00*

I assumed I knew why the gown had been purchased. However, why is it being sold without having been worn? Where is the groom? Is he perhaps the man with the boots?

One thing was certain. These were two people for whom things had changed. Plans had been made but things have changed.

When the winds of change blow through our lives, leaving in their path disappointments and regrets, we are usually faced with two questions. First, now that things have changed, what can I believe? Second, since things have changed, who can I trust?

When things change, I can still believe in the goodness of God and the unchanging Word of God. God's word about His sacrificial love for me and His forgiving grace is still true and has not changed. When things change, I can still trust God because His steadfast love for me cannot be swept away with stormy or shifting circumstances, but will always remain the same.

A man sells the boots. A woman sells the gown; but to the heart of the believer comes this blessed assurance: *"His steadfast love endures forever.*

 Lord, in a world of uncertainty, when things change, please remind me of that which is everlasting. Thank You for Your steadfast love and Your changeless grace and mercy.

 Swift to its close ebbs out life's little day;
Earth's joys grow dim, its glories pass away;
Change and decay in all around I see—
O Thou Who changeth not, abide with me.

Postal Dilemma

Luke 16:13
No man can serve two masters...

James 1:8
He is a double-minded man, unstable in all his ways.

When I go to the post office, I try to be a good citizen and do what is required of me. Lately, I find myself looking around to see if anyone is watching and hope not to be arrested for the way I mail my letters.

For quite some time, life was simple. There were two slots for mailing letters. Over the first slot the sign said, "local mail." I understood this and placed local mail there. Over the second slot the sign said, "out of town mail." I understood this too and compliance was a simple matter. Recently, the government has created a predicament for me. Now the sign over the first slot says, "Place all mail here." I could do this, but the sign over the second slot also says, "Place all mail here."

Herein lies the difficulty. If I place all of my mail in the first slot, I am not in compliance with the demand of the second slot that also asks for all my mail. I want to be a good law abiding citizen and I don't want to be seen as mutinous but the government is asking the impossible of me.

The world wants my life. If it cannot have all of it, it may compromise and demand only a part of it. Here is another problem. Jesus demands all of my life. He does not call me to part time devotion. His terms like cross bearing and self-denial leave no room for any of *my mail* to go elsewhere.

 Lord, You know how unstable I am. Please forgive my double-mindedness and lead me to so love You that I may truly sing, "All to Jesus I surrender. All to Him I freely give."

 Love so amazing, so divine,
Demands my soul, my life, my all.

Changing Underwear

Psalm 51:7
Purge me with hyssop, and I shall be clean;
Wash me, and I shall be whiter than snow.

The captain said to the first mate, "There is a foul odor on this ship. See that the men change their underwear.

The first mate said to the crew, "The captain says you are to change your underwear. John, you change with Joe. Bob, you change with Jim."

When I am made aware that changes need to be made in my life, there are options. The world offers me a wide range of alternatives. I can exchange my sense of insignificance for attention- seeking practices and unreasonable demands on others. I can exchange my loneliness for some unwholesome relationships. I can trade my confusion regarding directions I should take for foolish guides. I can change the haunting aware-ness of my guilt for a plethora of meaningless explana-tions and feeble excuses.

Unfortunately, those options leave me no better and no cleaner than before. Finding that the above choices can never bring about the change that I need, I can turn to the Savior in repentance and ask Him to make me clean.

Lord, the changes that I would make on my own will never make me what You have called me to be. I yield this sin stained life to You and ask that You "wash me and I shall be whiter than snow."

 Whiter than snow, yes, whiter than snow Now wash me and I shall be whiter than snow.

So You Won't Get Struck By Lightning

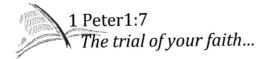

1 Peter 1:7
The trial of your faith...

One morning in 1940, several of us were standing by a West Texas road waiting for the school bus when a storm arose. A fierce wind was blowing and the thunder and lightning increased. Mrs. Jones, who lived near the bus stop ran out and yelled, "You young'uns get in this here house!" When we got inside, some of us sat on the bed in the front room. Others sat in chairs or on the floor. Mrs. Jones ran through the house gathering up pillows. She thrust one into the arms of each of us and commanded; "Hold on to those feather pillows so you won't get struck by lightning."

And you know something? It worked. Not one of us was struck by lightning. Since then, I've done some extensive research regarding this matter. (I talked with nine people.) Not one of them was ever struck by lightning while holding a feather pillow. Is this a system that really works, Or has it not yet been tested?

Like the incident with the pillows, some men have a tendency to develop their own survival systems, and they may call it their faith. It may be a verse from a song, a familiar saying, someone else's theories, a vague hunch, or a special feeling. They rely on this system for life here and the hereafter. Will it really work in a crisis? Will it really work when it is tested?

Lord, while others offer a variety of untested solutions for life's difficulties, please remind me that You are my only hope.

My hope is built on nothing less
Than Jesus' blood and righteousness.
I dare not trust the sweetest frame
But wholly lean on Jesus' name.

Holding On To Mama

John 13:1
... having loved His own which were in the world, He loved them unto the end.

During the revival in our rural church in 1941, one night the evangelist preached a sermon on hell and no one wanted to go there. The next night, he preached about Heaven and everyone wanted to go there. The following morning, my brother, Frank, and I were out past the barn discussing this and wondering if we would get into heaven. Frank very solemnly said, "I think I'll just hold on to Mama."

In later years, Frank learned that heaven is gained by grace through faith and in the years that followed, he lived out that faith. Still, I saw him "hold onto Mama" when she was in her nineties, in the hospital, and helpless. Each morning on the way to work he would bring her a biscuit from Grandy's. After work in the evening, he and his wife, Nelda, would spend most of the evening in her hospital room, doing a number of things to make her more comfortable and talking with her even when she could not communicate.

I once read an article by an airhead psychologist who wrote about "The Art Of Letting Go." She seemed to suggest that relationships should be considered to be temporary and can be discarded like paper plates, paper cups and other disposable items. I wished that someone had written about "The Art Of Holding On." There are those who can tell you how to let go. If you want to know how to hold on, ask Frank. He knows how. I think he learned it from the Savior Who said, *No one can snatch them out of My Father's hand.*

 Lord, forgive my spasmodic faithfulness to You. Thank You for Your constant faithfulness to me.

 O love that will not let me go. I rest my weary soul in Thee

The Diploma

1 Corinthians 13:2
And if I ... understand all mysteries and all knowledge, ... but have not love, I am nothing.

Philippians 3:10
That I may know Him.

Being justifiably proud of their academic accomplishments, the folks at the Police station all hung their college diplomas on their walls. Instead of hanging his college diploma, my brother, Frank, chose to hang his elementary school certificate. I believe this placed the matters of learning and knowledge in a more proper perspective. While in college, he studied some advanced matters, but it was in elementary school that he learned the basics. Sadly, some of us have had such an intense longing to be seen as intelligent and sophisticated that we have forgotten the basics. The basic truths are quite simple. We are sinners. God loves sinners. Christ died for sinners and by faith in Him we are forgiven and belong to Him forever. He longs for a close relationship with us and invites us to know Him intimately.

Lord, when I long for an understanding of complex matters, teach me to rejoice in the simple basics.

 More about Jesus would I know
More of His grace to others show
More of His saving fullness see
More of His love Who died for me.

Knocking For Love

Ephesians 1:4
He hath chosen us in him before the foundation of the world, that we should be holy and without blame before him in love.

You would have to understand the culture of rural west Texas in 1940. In a community made up primarily of Baptists and Methodists who strongly disapproved of dancing, the social life of the area was still not diminished. There were always the parties. Because of the limited population, ages of the attendees ranged all the way from twelve to eighteen.

One of the most popular games was *Knocking For Love*. The boys would stand outside while the girls on the inside numbered off. Then, one of the boys would knock on the door and someone on the inside would call "Number, Please". The boy would call out a number. The girl with that number would come out and the two of them would walk around the house or the fifty yards or so to the mailbox and back. I guess you may consider that rather bland by today's cultural standards. However, there was always the suspense of not knowing with whom you would be paired. A couple with a considerable age difference would still be gracious to one another. Two very young kids might run all the way to the mail box and back. An older couple might walk more slowly and even hold hands. There were, of course, those who would try to manipulate the system. Billie Joy would tell one of the girls, "Please tell Taylor I'm number four."

Those parties were a long time ago, but in a sense, the suspense still remains. Who wants to spend time with me? Who cares about me? Who would call my number? Jesus removes the anxiety regarding such matters with the announcement that *I have chosen you.*

Scripture tells us that *God demonstrates His love for us in that while we were yet sinners, Christ died for us.*

 Lord, when I become anxious about how much I matter to others, please remind me that You loved me and chose me. Amen

 Jesus Loves me.
  This I know.

Ordaining A Dog

Ephesians 3:7
By God's grace and mighty power, I have been given the privilege of serving Him by spreading this Good News.

I once knew a man whose verbal attacks were usually cruel, obscene and sometimes rather creative. Once when I was the object of one of his venomous tirades, he said, "So, you call yourself a preacher! I think I'll ordain my dog." Frankly, I had been questioning and sometimes doubting my qualifications for ministry. When one considers his own disobedience, half-hearted service and limited understanding of the things of God, can he ever assume the sacred right to serve a holy God?

Instead, God chose things the world considers foolish in order to shame those who think they are wise. And he chose things that are powerless to shame those who are powerful. God chose things despised by the world, things counted as nothing at all and used them to bring to nothing what the world considers important. As a result, no one can ever boast in the presence of God. (1 Corinthians 1:27-29) (NLT)

Lord, what an awesome thing it is to consider that a holy God like You would grant the high and sacred privilege of service to a sinner like me. Forgive me for being less than my calling deserves.

 Rise up of O men of God!
Have done with lesser things.
Give heart and mind and soul and strength
To serve the King of Kings.

Carrying Sandals

Matthew 3:11
*He who is coming after me is mightier than I,
Whose sandals I am not worthy to carry.*

How is it that, even in the service of the Master, one can pout and fret over a lack of status, praise or recognition? We have been given the holy privilege of serving One so great that just carrying His sandals is an honor beyond anything for which we could ever be considered worthy. To carry His sandals would be an honor beyond anything we could ever ask, hope or deserve.

While the world honors and praises people for that which is far less significant, I know of no one who has ever been made famous or highly honored by this world because of his unique ability to carry sandals.

Lord, teach me to accept any assignment You may give me with joy and gratitude. Remind me that any task You may give me is a holy privilege. Teach me to celebrate the honor of serving You. Lead me to handle my task in such a way that one day I may hear You say, "Well Done!"

*O Master, let me walk with Thee
In lowly paths of service free"*

Redneck Horse Racing

Matthew 16:2
He answered and said to them, "When it is evening you say, 'It will be fair weather, for the sky is red; and in the morning, 'It will be foul weather today, for the sky is red and threatening.' Hypocrites! You know how to discern the face of the sky, but you cannot discern the signs of the times."

Bubba called Billy Bob and announced that he had purchased a racehorse. Billy Bob responded, "How 'bout that? I bought one too." They decided that they would meet each Saturday morning at Johnson's pasture for a race.

At the end of the first race, there was confusion as to who owned which horse. This led to a heated argument before each took a horse and went home.

The next Saturday Bubba decided to avoid confusion by trimming his horse's mane. Unfortunately Billy Bob had done the same thing. So, at the end of the race there was more confusion and an argument. On the third Saturday, Bubba cut most of the hair off his horse's tail but this did no good because Billy Bob had done the same thing.

They decided that they needed professional help, so they contacted the agricultural department at L.S.U. An equine expert arrived and after checking eyes, teeth, and hooves he found no significant difference. In a final effort to find a distinguishable difference, he decided to measure the horses. To everyone's surprise, they found that the black horse was taller than the white one.

LESSON: Don't overlook the obvious.

Unfortunately in our heated arguments over trivial matters, we have overlooked some things that are as plain as black and white. Our petty arguments may cause us to overlook these awesome truths.

1. *God loves us.*
2. *We are sinners.*
3. *God still loves us and has given His Son to redeem us.*

His sacrificial love and forgiving grace are plain as black and white. This is enough.

 Lord, forgive me for times when obsessing over secondary matters has caused me to forget Your measureless sacrificial love.

 I need no other argument.
I need no other plea.
It is enough that Jesus died.
And that He died for me.

Captain Hook

James 4:3
You have not because you ask amiss.

Not all of my prayers have been answered in ways that I would have preferred. In His infinite wisdom, God knew that there are some things I would not have handled well. He knew that, more than an abundance of things, I needed to know how to trust Him to provide all I need. He knew that, more than recognition and praise, I needed to praise Him.

Anything outside these parameters may prove to be destructive.

A pirate was greeted by an old friend who said, "I see you have a wooden leg." The pirate said, "I lost my leg in a battle, but with this wooden leg I am fine." The friend then noticed the hook where the right hand had been. The pirate explained that in another fight, someone cut off his right hand but with the hook he was fine. He said, "Just feel how sharp that claw is!" Then the friend asked about the eye patch. The pirate said, "In a card game, one of the men got mad and spit tobacco into my eye." The friend asked, "How did the tobacco cause you to lose your eye?" The pirate explained, "It was my first day with the hook."

Lord, You know me. You know my desires. You also know what is best. Teach me to be content with what You choose to give.

 Once earthly joys I craved
Sought peace and rest.
Now Thee alone I seek.
Give what is best.

Obnoxious Honors

Psalm 133:1
Behold, how good and how pleasant it is for brethren to dwell together in unity.

There is a particular species of elk that you may find interesting. However, if you choose to pet this African elk, it is best not to touch his head. When two combative males fight, if one severely wounds his opponent, he takes the droppings from his defeated foe and smears them on the front of His head as a badge of honor and as a testimony to his prowess. His victory has not made him more attractive, only more obnoxious.

When there is a conflict within an organization, a family, or the Body Of Christ, one may win and get his way, but where is the joy if the "winner" has only created an unpleasant atmosphere for those around him?

Lord, teach us to treasure this precious thing called fellowship that we may fulfill Your command to love one another.

Blest be the tie that binds
Our hearts in Christian love
The fellowship of kindred minds
Is like to that above.

Gorilla Wrestling

Psalm 139:11
*If I say, Surely the darkness shall cover me;
even the night shall be light about me.*

The Friday night patrons at the local restaurant had become exasperated because each Friday evening while they were eating with friends, Bubba, the town bully would come in. He would flirt with the women and try to pick fights with the men. One day they decided they had endured this long enough. The next Friday afternoon, they went to the zoo and rented a gorilla. They placed the gorilla in the back room of the restaurant. When Bubba came strutting in, they told him a lady wanted to meet him in the back room. As Bubba swaggered into the room they turned out the lights. At first there was a long period of silence. Then, they heard furniture being shoved around. Then they heard the crash of broken furniture as chairs were being smashed. Finally there was silence again. When Bubba walked out bruised, bleeding and with torn clothes, he said, "Giving an ugly woman a fur coat doesn't make her any nicer."

I would like to appear better than I really am. I may try to dress myself more elegantly, but this will not make me a better person. I may find a dark room in which to hide, but I am still who I am. My only hope is in the forgiving grace of God Who promised to change me. Scripture tells us that if any man be in Christ, he is a new creation. Old things are passed away. Behold, all things are made new.

Lord, thou hast searched me and known me. Since you already know me, give me the faith to step out into the light.

When He shall come with trumpet sound,
Oh, may I then in Him be found,
Dressed in His righteousness alone,
Faultless to stand before the throne!

Landing in Slobovia

Philippians 3:20
For our citizenship is in heaven, from which we also eagerly wait for the Savior, the Lord Jesus Christ.

The plane made an emergency landing in bitterly cold Lower Slobovia where the men were mean, ugly and unpleasant and the women were meaner, uglier and even more unpleasant.

The pilot cautioned the passengers that they should remain close to one another and to the crew because they would soon be going home.

One passenger ignored the warning and began visiting the nearby Slobovian village. For protection, he enrolled in a Slobovian martial arts class. Seeking approval and acceptance by the Slobovians, he enrolled in a Slobovian language class. He even began to participate in their games. While other passengers encouraged one another and shared their excitement regarding anticipated reunions with loved ones, he was preoccupied with trying to fit in where he did not belong.

Lord, forgive me for neglecting my fellowship with my "fellow passengers." Forgive me for my attempts to fit in where I really do not belong.

This world is not my home
I'm just a passing through.
The angels beckon me
From Heaven's open door
And I can't feel at home
In this world anymore.

Wisdom In Busy Places

Proverbs 1:20-21
*Lady Wisdom goes out in the street and shouts.
At the town center she makes her speech. In
the middle of the traffic she takes her stand. At
the busiest corner she calls out...* (MSG)

For too long, we have believed the myth that in better circumstances we would be better people. We have assumed that in a less frantic atmosphere, we would meditate on God's Word and in a more serene atmosphere, we would discover the wisdom we need. The truth is that God's desire is to speak to us in the middle of life as it is. In the middle of the traffic Wisdom takes her stand.

The issue is not my surroundings, but a willingness to hear and heed what God has to say.

Lord, while I have been waiting for a change in my circumstances, I have neglected Your invitation to come to You that You may change me. Please speak that I may hear even in the middle of the busy traffic of my life.

*From the fears that long have bound us
Free our hearts to faith and praise
Grant us wisdom. Grant us courage
For the living of these days*

Hand Grenades

1 Chronicles 4:10
And Jabez called on the God of Israel saying,
"Oh, that You would bless me indeed... and that
You would keep me from evil, that I may not
cause pain."

Three Slobovians found three hand grenades on a street in New York City. After a lengthy discussion regarding what should be done, they decided to place them in a bag and take them to the police station. While they were on their way, one of them asked, "What if one of them explodes before we get there?" Another replied, "We'll just lie and say we only found two."

Sometimes, in choosing a course of action, we can be so caught up in explanations and excuses (even dishonest ones) that we give little thought to actual consequences. Those explanations and excuses cannot undo the pain we have brought to others or to ourselves by our destructive choices.

Lord, forgive my foolish choices. Lead me to so love
You that your tenderness and compassion would
mold my decisions that I might not cause pain.

Take my hands and let them move
At the impulse of Thy love

Accepting New Leadership

Joshua 1:16-17
So they answered Joshua, saying, "All that you command us we will do, and wherever you send us we will go. Just as we heeded Moses in all things, so we will heed you. Only the Lord your God be with you, as He was with Moses."

After forty years of leadership, Moses is gone. The Reubenites and Gadites demonstrate a loyalty that transcends allegiance to a past leader. They display a commitment that transcends loyalty to family. They exhibit a faithfulness that surpasses concern for their property east of the Jordan. Their loyalty was not just to a person but to a cause. They asked for only one thing to remain unchanged: the presence of the Lord in the life of their leader.

In the midst of changes in my surroundings and circumstances, I need leadership. Jesus invites me to follow Him and trust Him to lead.

Lord, when my circumstances change, there may be choices and decisions to be made. I turn to You and ask that You be my Leader.

He leadeth me: O Blessed thought!
O words of heavenly comfort fraught!
What 'er I do, where 'er I be,
Still 'tis God's hand that leadeth me

Put Away Your Sword

Matthew 26:52
"Put away your sword," Jesus told him... (NLT)

Philippians 4:19
And my God shall supply all your need
according to His riches in glory by Christ Jesus.

Discipleship will always be a matter of putting away. To know the peace He offers, I must put away my own weapons with which I would fight those who oppose me. I must put away my preconceived notions about Him that I may truly know Him. I may be asked to put away my own agenda that His plan and purpose may be accomplished. He may ask me to put away my own methods that His work may be done His way.

When all these things have been put away from me, I am left with only Him and His promise that all my needs will be met according to His riches in Glory by Christ Jesus.

Lord, forgive my tight grip on those things that have mattered too much to me.

All to Jesus I surrender
All to Him I freely give.

Jesus Changed My Life

2 Corinthians 5:17
Therefore, if any anyone is in Christ, he is a new creation; old things have passed away; behold, all things have become new.

Recently, at the corner of Loop Road and Hwy 165, I saw an old van that could only be described as a moving collection of safety violations. The fenders were rusty. Duct tape covered a broken window. The bumper was hanging at a crooked angle and smoke billowed from the exhaust. Another thing caught my eye. On that loose bumper was a bumper sticker that said *Jesus Changed My Life.*

At first I was rather annoyed because it seems that if anyone has had a life changing experience and wants to give Jesus the credit for it, he should drive a Ferrari, a Lincoln, or at least an Oldsmobile. As I pondered this, it occurred to me that I never saw the man. I only saw the vehicle. It had not occurred to me that the difference was not in what he owned but who he had become. What mattered was not my impression of him but the Savior's love for him.

Lord, forgive my foolish ways of measuring Your children. Forgive my excessive concern with what belongs to me and remind me that belonging to You matters more. Teach me to celebrate being new, that others may know that Jesus changed my life.

 What a wonderful change in my life has been wrought Since Jesus came into my heart.

Bartimaeus

Mark 10:46-52

And throwing aside his garment, he rose and came to Jesus. So Jesus answered and said to him, " What do you want Me to do for you?" The blind man said to Him, "Rabboni, that I may receive my sight." Then Jesus said to him, "Go your way; your faith has made you well." And immediately he received his sight and followed Jesus on the road.

John 8:12

Then Jesus spoke to them again, saying, "I am the light of the world. He who follows Me shall not walk in darkness, but have the light of life."

Picture a blind man sitting beside the road with a blanket draped across his shoulders. He sits there with his tin cup and cane. His daily occupation is that of calling attention to his problem, hoping for a few coins in his cup. On this day, he dares to ask for more than small change in his cup. He will ask for a big change in his life.

As he begins to cry out for mercy, there were those who tried to silence him, but he cries even louder. The good news is that we do not need the permission of an uncaring world to ask the Savior for mercy.

BARTIMAEUS

Lord of mercy, can it be
That you should care for one like me?
Here in darkness I still wait
Mid uncaring crowds at Jericho's gate.

I long for sights of trees and skies
Kept from me by blinded eyes
But these blind eyes now turn to You
And hope and ask that You will do
What others say that you have done.
Help me now, Oh David's Son.

O mercy, boundless as the sea
I run to Him, He's calling me
I leave my blanket, cup and cane.
He'll touch me and I'll see again.

*Lord, You know the darkness that robs me of
the glorious things You want me to see. Please
forgive me for simply trying to adapt to my
blindness with the coins of this world. Please
give me the faith to follow You that I might have
the light of life.*

*Amazing grace! How sweet the sound!
I once was lost, but now I'm found!
Was blind, but now I see.*

The Uniform

Matthew 16:24
Then Jesus said to His disciples, "If anyone desires to come after Me, let him deny himself, and take up his cross, and follow Me."

He was considered to be one of the "characters" in Martin County. He never harmed anyone. He was never unkind to anyone. He simply did not fit in with our West Texas society. I don't think anyone was ever unkind to him; but neither do I think he had any friends.

I suppose you could say that he "marched to the sound of a different drummer." He lived out past our farm and every morning he would walk the eight miles to our small town. When he arrived, he would go the Rexall Drug store and drink a milk shake. After finishing the milk shake, he would stand on the corner for a while. Then, he would walk the eight miles back home.

When World War II began, many of the local young men went into military service. When they would come home wearing their uniforms, folks would gather around them, admire the uniform and tell the young soldiers or sailors how proud they were of them. So the "misfit" joined the army and received his uniform. Two weeks later, the army sent him home because of his *"failure to adjust to military life".* When he came home he brought his uniform.

Whenever there was a basketball game, football game or other community event, he would always appear wearing his cherished uniform. As he paraded up and down before the stands, he marched with his shoulders back, taking long strides and swinging his arms. Thus, everyone would know he was a soldier.

I really find it hard to be critical of him when I recall those times when I concerned myself more with my image as a *Christian Soldier*, than with the genuineness of my own devotion to the Lord. After all, strutting is easier than cross bearing and dressing up is easier than kneeling down. Also, making noise is so much more convenient than making costly commitments.

Jesus never told us to try to dress up like soldiers. He simply commanded us to take up a cross, follow Him and lay down our lives for Him.

 Lord, thank You for honoring me by calling me Your servant. Forgive me for the times when looking like a servant mattered more than being one. Forgive my reluctance to bear Your cross.

 Am I a soldier of the cross,
  A follower of the Lamb?

Just Doug's Dad

Luke 11:2
So He said to them, " When you pray, say:
Our Father in heaven, hallowed be Your name."

Today I met a man who introduced himself simply as Doug's dad. He never spoke of his own title, position, profession or accomplishment. He was pleased to be known as just "Doug's Dad" I knew Doug and knew he had reason be very proud of his son.

God could well be known as Creator of a vast universe or Maker of mountains, rainbows and sunsets but He delights in calling Himself our Father.

The Old Testament speaks of Him as The Exalted One, the Lord of Hosts, the Holy One and many other names that speak of His power, glory and majesty. When David thought of His protection he called God his Fortress. When he thought of the joy He brings he called God his Song. Remembering his tender care, he said, *The Lord is my Shepherd.*

When Jesus came, He called God His Father and then told us that we could call His Father our Father too. Of all the majestic names He could be called, He seems to take most delight in being called our Father.

Lord, what an awesome thing to consider that even with my faults and failures, You still delight in calling me Your son and invite me to call You my Father.

Children of the heavenly Father
Safely in His bosom gather
Nesting bird nor star in Heaven
Such a refuge e're was given.

God His own doth tend and nourish
In His holy courts they flourish
From all evil things He spares them
In His mighty arms He bears them.

Mirrors, Bibles and Tigress Perfume *

Each year, the children at the Baptist Children's Home were asked to write "Christmas Letters" indicating things they would like to receive for Christmas. The housemother from one of the cottages told me that five of the teenage girls had all wanted the same things. They each suggested they would like to receive a Living Bible, a makeup mirror and some Tigress perfume.

On the night of the Christmas parties, as I entered the cottage, it was obvious that they all had the Tigress Perfume. They each also received nice makeup mirrors and the copies of the Living Bible.

In a sense, this is what Louisiana Baptists had already been providing for them. It gave them an opportunity to take a new look at themselves and discover a beauty they did not know was there. As with the perfume, it taught them how to change the atmosphere around them. It also gave them an opportunity to learn of the love of the Savior.

I don't know what became of the Bibles, mirrors and perfume, but I know that even today, they live lives indicating that they discovered real beauty in themselves. They change the atmosphere around them through their radiant Christian lives. They also celebrate and share the Savior's love they discovered in His word.

Shirley, Rosie, Pam, Betty Jo and Lillian, I'm so proud of you.

* First Published in "Dinner Bells, Pecan Shells And True Tales from the Home" A publication of the Louisiana Baptist Children's Home.

Circumstantial Praise

Psalm 137: 1-4
By the rivers of Babylon, there we sat down, yea, we wept when we remembered Zion. We hung our harps upon the willows in the midst of it. For there those who carried us away captive asked of us a song, And those who plundered us requested mirth, saying, "Sing us one of the songs of Zion!" How shall we sing the Lord's song in a foreign land?

Luke 10:20
Nevertheless do not rejoice in this, that the spirits are subject to you, but rather rejoice because your names are written in heaven.

Our team won and so we celebrated. However, the next week our team lost and there was no celebration. I had a good day and was glad. The next day was not so good and so there was less gladness. During the bright days, we celebrated with music. Then dark days came and we hung up the instruments, saying, *"how can we sing...?"*

The disciples returned from their mission rejoicing over their successes. Life was good and they were victorious in their efforts. It was good to stand in the winner's circle and celebrate their victories. Jesus saw beyond the ecstasy of the moment and knew that trouble would come and they would be persecuted, mistreated and killed. He knew that times and circumstances would change for them. He also knows that our circumstances and our successes are all temporary. He knew that His friends needed to celebrate that which lasted. He told them to celebrate, *because your names are written in Heaven.* This is a solid changeless fact. No matter how present circumstances may change, we can still look beyond these and rejoice as we celebrate a changeless love and a changeless hope in that which will come.

Far too often, I have rejoiced in some things that will not last. Please forgive my preoccupation with the temporal and teach me to celebrate that which is eternal.

When we all get to heaven,
What a day of rejoicing that will be!
When we all see Jesus,
We'll sing and shout the victory!

Three Rich Kids

Mark 8:36
*For what will it profit a man if he gains the
whole world, and loses his own soul.*

It was In the summer of 1940. My brother, Frank was seven, I was nine, and my older brother, Troy, was eleven. Except for Sundays, we spent our summer days in the fields. These days were not wasted because we developed a work ethic and had some very stimulating philosophical discussions. One day our conversation turned to the field of economics as we came up with the great idea that it would be a great thing if rocks were what counted instead of money. I claimed the rocks out past the swings at the school. Troy claimed the rocks behind the grocery store and Frank claimed a pile of rocks behind the barn. No one had ever enjoyed such wealth. Bill Gates, Warren Buffet and Donald Trump were paupers compared to us. As we walked down those cotton rows celebrating our wealth, we determined that we would not have to go to school any more and we could go to town every Saturday. Later, our conversation moved into the area of animal psychology. (Were pigs dumber than chickens?)

Suddenly Frank threw his hat into the air and shouted, "I get the rocks at the Reeves place!" Troy and I stood there in dumbfounded amazement. The Reeves farm was nothing but rocks. They had rocks in their road, in their pasture, in their front yard and even in the cow pens.

This just would not do. The youngest of us was a thousand times richer than we were. We told him that he could not have those rocks. He said they were his because he claimed them first. Soon reasoning turned into name-calling and then into pushing, shoving and hitting. I don't remember if or how the matter was resolved. I only remember three very angry little boys hitting and hurting one another out of concern for some rocks that were of no value, even though we pretended that they were, and were not really ours even though we claimed them.

How sad it would be to near the end of life and look back remembering anger and frustration over our excessive concerns for other things that were of very little value though we thought they were and were not really ours even though we claimed them?

 Lord, forgive me for allowing the things of this world to blind me to that which really matters.

 I'd rather have Jesus than silver or gold.
I'd rather be His than have riches untold.

Tuxedos and Other Temporary Honors

Mark 15:17
And they clothed Him with purple; and they twisted a crown of thorns, put it on His head and began to salute Him.

Mark 15:20
And when they had mocked Him, they took the purple off Him, put His own clothes on Him.

Psalms 10:16
The Lord is King forever and ever.

John went off to college and left his brother, Bill, to work with their father on the farm.

Years later, Bill called John and informed him that Pa had died and the funeral would be next Friday. John said his many responsibilities as a corporate executive made it impossible for him to attend, but said that Bill was to spare no expense in planning a first class funeral. He said, "just have the funeral home send me the bill and I'll pay for everything."

A month later, John received a bill and immediately sent a check.

The next month, there was another bill for six hundred dollars. John assumed that this was a charge overlooked in the original bill, so he sent another check.

However, every month, there was another six hundred dollar charge. After a year of sending a check each month he called his brother and asked about the recurring charge. Bill explained, "You know Pa never had anything to wear except his overalls so we rented him a tuxedo."

The royal robe the soldiers placed on Jesus was to be worn briefly while they mocked Him. All too soon, they removed this dubious honor.

Lord, please forgive the temporary nature of any honor I may bestow upon You. Forgive me for forgetting that Thine is the kingdom forever.

Oh, worship the King, all glorious above.
Oh, gratefully sing His power and His love;
Our Shield and Defender, the Ancient of Days,
Pavilioned in splendor, and girded with praise.

Don Quixote

1 John 3:1
Behold what manner of love the Father has bestowed on us, that we should be called children of God!

More than four centuries ago, Miguel de Cervantes wrote a novel about Don Quixote. There was a senile old man who in his deranged state imagined himself to be a knight. Taking a discarded washbasin that he regarded as a golden helmet, he rode off to do battle for truth, beauty and justice. When he came to a vile smelling, run down tavern, in his confused state, he saw it as the great castle. Inside this "castle" he met cheap, course and trashy Aldonza. In his unbalanced state, he saw her as the pure sweet high-born lady of the "castle." He called her Dulcenea. (Sweet Lady.)

She protested that she was no lady and described her sordid occupation. He protested, "Not so, my lady. You are Dulcenea."

After he fought some of her customers for her dubious honor, life could never be the same for her again. She became what she was called. When asked about the change in her life, she replied, "He called me by a different name." Some of us spend a lifetime living down to the names we have been called. There are names like failure, weak, unlovable, or worthless. Then the

Savior came and took your hand. He was neither confused nor blind, but through eyes of love He called you "Beloved." To show you that there was no mistake in His love for you, He carried a cross to Calvary and suffered there, revealing a love that could never be questioned or denied.

 Lord, You know the names I have allowed the world to call me. You know the names that in my despair I have called myself. Thank You for calling me Your friend.

 There's a new name written down in glory.
And it's mine.

Moving On

Numbers 21:10
Now the children of Israel moved on and camped in Oboth.

The book of Numbers is the wonderful story of God's tender leadership of His people to the promised land. It is the glorious story of the claiming of the promised inheritance. It is also the shameful story of the grumbling and complaining of a discontented people. It is a story of fiery serpents, suffering, confession, intercession, grace and healing.

It is also a story of moving on. Some would have camped there with their guilt, only to be haunted each day with memories of their past sin. Others would have remained there to memorialize their pain, suffering and grief, allowing it to remain the central focus of their lives. Still others would have wanted to remain in the wilderness with their memories of the spectacular event involving the brass serpent and the moment of healing. However, the scripture says the children of Israel moved on.

Lord, please remind me that each day is not the total history of my life, but another step in a glorious journey. Do not allow me to be trapped by issues of the moment, but take my hand and lead me so that whatever may come, it may be said of me that I moved on.

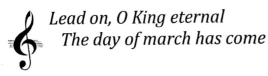

Lead on, O King eternal
  The day of march has come

Donkeys To Ride

Judges 10:3
After him arose Jair, a Gileadite; and he judged Israel twenty- two years. Now he had thirty sons who rode on thirty donkeys.

Mother: "Tell me about Jimmy. What's he like?"

Daughter: "He's cute and he drives a convertible."

In the scriptures, we are told of some men who are remembered for risks taken, battles fought, wise leadership and responses to the needs around them. We are also told of their failed efforts and losses. Jair and his children are remembered only for the donkeys they rode.

It is a sobering thought to consider how we will be remembered. The car, the house, and other superficial testimonies of our success may matter little more than the donkeys ridden by Jair and his family.

Someone has said, "He who dies with the most toys wins." Someone wiser rewrote the comment by saying, "He who dies with most toys dies."

 Lord, forgive me for those things that have mattered more than they should. Only as You

*continually restructure my value system and re-
order my priorities will my life have the meaning
You have planned.*

 *I'd rather have Jesus than silver or gold.
I'd rather be His than have riches untold.*

Fictitious Wife

1 John 4:10
In this is love: not that we have loved God, but that He loved us and sent His Son to be the atoning sacrifice for our sins. (NET)

When I arrived at the military base in Salzburg Austria in 1955, three other men arrived at the same time and the four of us were assigned to the same four-man cubicle in the barracks. As we were unpacking, I showed the other men a picture of Letha. They in turn each took eight by ten photos from their duffel bags and introduced the group to their wives. Keith, the youngest, showed us a picture of a strikingly beautiful young lady and said, "This is Helen, my wife." The picture was signed, *"To my darling with all my love, Helen."*

In the following days, our conversations often turned to the subject of our wives. Keith would join in the conversation, telling us about the music Helen liked, what Helen cooked, and places he and Helen had gone together.

After several weeks of receiving no mail from home, Keith told us that he really did not have a wife. His girlfriend had broken up with him just before he left the states. The picture was stolen from someone on the ship on the journey over. He explained the theft by saying, "On the ship, it was like it is here. Everyone else had someone and I didn't have anyone."

We live in a sad and lonely world where so many people have no one and settle for fantasies and pretend relationships with movie stars, TV personalities or Facebook friends.

The good news is that the Savior Who was called a Friend of sinners came into this lonely and hurting world and offered us His forgiving grace and a close intimate eternal relationship with Him.

 Thank You for the real and lasting love You made so plain at the cross.

 Jesus what a friend for sinners!
Jesus lover of my soul.
Hallelujah! What A Savior!
Hallelujah! What a Friend!

Washington Needs Me

John 21:21-22
Peter, seeing him, said to Jesus, "But Lord, what about this man?" Jesus said to him, "If I will that he remain till I come, what is that to you? You follow Me."

Wouldn't it be great if I could go to Washington, call the president and all the congressmen together and persuade them to confess and abandon their deceptive practices, speak only the truth and do only that which is right and good? As of yet, neither the president nor members of congress have called me. Since they are not likely to call for my help, perhaps I should put aside my dream and deal with present realities in my own life. I should bow in repentance and place my own ambition and unworthy motives in the hands of the Savior, claim His forgiving grace and follow Him.

Lord, you know my disappointment with some other people. Give me the wisdom to place matters that are out of my reach in Your hands, that I might follow You.

Jesus calls us by thy mercies,
Savior, may we hear Thy call.
Give our hearts to Thine obedience,
Serve and love Thee most of all.

I Cried Last Night

Romans 12:15
Rejoice with those who rejoice, and weep with those who weep...

Isaiah 53:4
Surely He has borne our griefs and carried our sorrows.

2 Timothy 1:4
Greatly desiring to see thee, being mindful of thy tears.

I Cried Last Night

I cried last night and felt the shame
Of self revealing tears that came
Coursing down my burning cheek
And told the world that I was weak.

Through dark corridors of my mind
Marched haunting memories of every kind
That taunt, accuse, deride and blame
Me for my failure, loss and shame.

I cried last night and then You came
You held my hand and spoke my name
Now I know I'll be alright
For You cried with me when I cried last night

Lord, when tears come, thank You for being mindful of them and sharing them. No wonder they called You a man of sorrows.

We share our mutual woes
Our mutual burdens bear
And often for each other flows
A sympathizing tear.

Out of the Synagogue

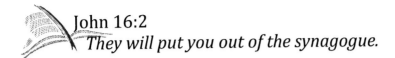

John 16:2
They will put you out of the synagogue.

I have my traditions, habits and practices. Some of my customary ways of doing things are very meaningful to me. I am reluctant to consider that these things may matter more than they should.

What if my walk with the Lord does not allow me to hold on to my ways and do what I have always done? What if my routine is disrupted? What If I am put out of "my synagogue?"

Will worship be less meaningful? Will service be less gratifying? Would I have the courage to consider that my acts of service may mean more to me than the One I serve. To become a servant of the Lord requires one to give up some bad habits. We may be required to give up some of our good ones too.

Lord, you know how much some of my patterns, habits and routines mean to me. Forgive me for those times when they mean too much. Give me such a love for You that even those things that I consider to be good can be surrendered to You.

All to Jesus, I surrender.
I surrender all.

God Bless The Cheerleaders

Proverbs 25:20
*Like vinegar on soda is one who sings songs to
a heavy heart.*

One year in the late 1960's or early 1970's, I was expected to attend all the Jr. High football games because
several of our boys from the Children's Home were on
the team. That was the year that our team established
what was possibly the worst record in all football history.

Each Thursday, I sat through a miserable night of
fumbles, sacks, interceptions and other mistakes. I
would sit there, wishing the clock would move faster
and bring the disaster to a merciful end. Yet, the pep
squad showed no lack of enthusiasm. When we were
intercepted, they would yell as if we had just made a
touchdown. When we fumbled, lost yardage, or were
humiliated in other ways, the cheerleaders jumped up
and down with seeming glee. I never understood their
chanting, "We're Number One! We're Number One!"

One of our girls was a cheerleader. The next afternoon
she stopped by my office and said, "I saw you at the
game last night. Wasn't it a great game?" I could only
reply "Our boys really tried."

She asked, "Did you see us cheerleaders?" Knowing she
was fishing for a compliment, I mentioned that they

showed lots of energy and enthusiasm. Then I just had to ask why they cheered so enthusiastically when we fumbled or were intercepted or why they chanted "We're Number One?" She replied, "We don't know about all that. We just lead the cheers." So my attitude toward cheerleaders was that these were simple minded airheads that really should not be out in public.

Years later, I was in the hospital emergency waiting room with some parents who were anxious about their injured daughter. While we were waiting, four cheerleaders came in wearing their cute little skirts, sweaters, and white tennis shoes. I was glad that at least they left their pom-poms in the car. My first reaction was that they were out of place. Then, I watched as they went to the patient's mother, wept with her and prayed with her. Thus, my next attitude toward cheerleaders was that perhaps some of them are OK.

Then, in 1998, I met Michelle. She was an attractive, vivacious cheerleader. She was also an outstanding scholar. I think she was senior class valedictorian. She was also an outstanding Christian witness at the school. In the weeks following her dad's death, I saw her comfort and strengthen her mother. She would pass up opportunities to hang out with friends because she felt her mom needed her.

Now I had concluded that not all cheerleaders are airheads.

A few years later, she spent time in Haiti ministering to hurting people. Today, she is an outstanding wife, mother, and servant of the Lord.

I must admit that my attitude toward cheerleaders has had to grow and change.

Could it be that my attitude toward some other folks needs improving?

 Lord, forgive me for judging others by surface appearances. Teach me to place such appearances in Your hands.

 Serve the Lord with gladness
Enter His courts with song.

It's Personal

Proverbs 14:10
*The heart knows its own bitterness,
and a stranger does not share its joy.*

Isaiah 53:4
*Surely He has borne our griefs and carried our
sorrows...*

Outside the family of God, I live in a world of strangers. Without "the tie that binds", I walk in isolation. My bitterness, my disappointments, my sorrow and my joy are my own. Yes, there may be friends or neighbors who stand ready to help and encourage; but without a sharing of the love of the Savior, at the very core of my being, I am alone.

However, the good news is that I do not have to bear my sorrow alone and my joy is multiplied as I am privileged to share it with others. This "Man Of Sorrows" has borne my grief and carried my sorrow.

*Lord, thank You for Your promise that I will never
be alone. Thank You for fellowship with my
brothers and sisters who along with You share
my pain and my joy.*

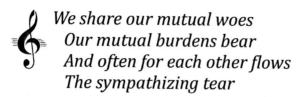

We share our mutual woes
Our mutual burdens bear
And often for each other flows
The sympathizing tear

Expensive Companionship

1 John 1:3
Truly our fellowship is with the Father and with His Son Jesus Christ.

During a political campaign, the president spoke at a fund raising dinner. For sixty five thousand dollars per plate, I could have met the president, eaten with Hollywood celebrities and hobnobbed with prominent politicians and other folks regarded by the world as important.

I passed up on that opportunity. I suppose you did too. If you were inclined to attend, would you still be haunted with a sense of your own insignificance?

The good news is that the Creator of the universe loves you. His Son has died for you and you are invited to become a member of God's family.

Lord, when I become anxious about how much I matter to others, please remind me that You loved me and chose me.

Jesus loves me. This I know.

Face To Face

2 John 1:12
I have much more to say to you, but I don't want to do it with paper and ink. For I hope to visit you soon and talk with you face to face. Then our joy will be complete.

After days of searching for a lost dog, a man placed an ad in the local paper. When his wife asked what the ad said, he replied, "Here Boy!"

In an increasingly impersonal world, clever face-book posts, concise tweets and newspaper ads may be effective in disseminating information, but they are woefully inadequate substitutes for words of love and encouragement that someone needs to hear you speak to them.

The impersonal seems safer because you do not have to risk being rebuked or rejected, but real healing and joy takes place with honest face to face conversation.

In the upper room, Jesus spoke of His strong desire to celebrate the passover with His friends. In the garden of Gethsemane, He shared the sorrow of His soul with His three closest friends.

When He called me to follow Him, it was in order that day by day we may converse personally with each other. *And He walks with me and He talks with me and He tells me I am His own.*

 Lord, forgive me for hiding in the impersonal when there are those that need the personal words of hope and encouragement You would have me speak.

 Speak to my heart Lord Jesus.
Speak that my soul may hear.
Speak to my heart Lord Jesus
Calm every doubt and fear.

Grace For A Losing Fighter

Ephesians 2:8-9
For by grace you have been saved through faith, and that not of yourselves; it is the gift of God, not of works, lest anyone should boast.

My career as a prizefighter ended shamefully and yet gloriously in October in 1941. Each year at the local Halloween carnival, when all the other games and attractions were shut down, everyone had to go outside and pay twenty five cents to get back inside to watch the boxing matches. My so-called friend, Elvis Fisher, suggested that we box. We would get in free and the winner would get a sheet of war stamps worth a dollar.

I was reluctant because I feared getting hurt, but he assured me that with those big gloves you didn't feel anything and he promised that we would not hit each other very hard. I'm sure his character has improved somewhat since 1941, but that night he lied.

When we got in the ring, he knocked me down several times, and at other times chased me around the ring hitting and hurting me. He won. He won the stamps. After the matches were over, while I was trying to keep from crying, one of the local men said, "I know what it's like. Here's a dime." Another handed me a quarter and said, "It's tough isn't it?" Several others stopped by, shook my hand and offered me encouragement and slipped me some coins. Elvis, the winner got the stamps worth one dollar. I went home with a pocket full of coins and a feeling of being understood by those neighboring farmers who knew what it was like to lose to drought, sand storms, and a number of other reasons for crop failures.

The winner earned the stamps and that's all he got. That's works.

This loser got even more. That's grace.

 Lord, I could never earn Your favor or my salvation. Thank You for Your freely given love.

 Amazing grace!
How sweet the sound!

Make My Day

Numbers 11:18
Sanctify yourselves for tomorrow...

Tomorrow is a part of my journey I have not yet traveled. I do not know what problems must be faced or what questions must be answered. I do not know what tasks must be completed, or what burdens must be carried. I'm not sure I will be wise enough for the problems or have the answers to the questions. I do not know if I will have the ability to complete the tasks or the strength to bear the burdens.

I must yield tomorrow to the Lord, but I may still be anxious if I have not yielded myself to Him too. Only as I am in fellowship with Him can I know that all will be well with me because He loves me and has the wisdom for the problems, the answers for the questions, (If I really need answers) and the strength for tasks and burdens. He also brings with Him His forgiving grace for my sin, and His love for my lonely heart. He will make tomorrow a day in which I can say,

This is the day the Lord has made.
We will rejoice and be glad in it.

Lord, go ahead. Make my day!

 But I know Who holds tomorrow.
And I know Who holds my hand.

Long Journeys and Heavy Loads

Luke 9:3
*And he said unto them, "Take nothing for your
journey, neither staves, nor scrip, neither
bread, neither money; neither have two coats
apiece."*

Over the years, my wife has grown weary of my saying,
"If a little does a little good, a lot will do a lot of good." I
don't know how or why it has taken me so long to learn
that this is not always true.

You stand at the courthouse steps in ninety-eight de-
gree weather because you are required to walk to the
courthouse in the next town. You are prepared for this
forty mile walk with a cane, a ham sandwich and a canteen.

Just before you begin walking, a bystander approach-
es you and says, "the water in that canteen may not
be enough. Carry this five gallon jug of water. Then he
says, "it's a long walk and that ham sandwich may not
be enough. Carry this eight pound ham, two pounds of
cheese and five loaves of bread."

Then he says, "I see you have only one cane. Canes do
get broken. Here are six more for you to carry." His final offer is a heavy overcoat. You remind him that the
temperature is ninety eight degrees, but he points out
that weather can be unpredictable and you should be

prepared in case you encounter a blizzard before the day is over.

You can carry the heavy load he offers, or trust your Guide Who promises to walk beside you and provide for all your needs.

 Lord, forgive me for choosing the heavy load of anxiety over Your promise to care for me. You are my Shepherd. I shall not want.

 I must tell Jesus all of my trials
I cannot bear these burdens alone.

When The Pope Died

Revelation 3:20
Behold, I stand at the door and knock. If anyone hears My voice and opens the door, I will come in to him and dine with him, and he with Me.

Recently the Pope died. Hundreds of thousands of people stood in line for as much as twenty hours just to walk swiftly by for a brief glimpse of his body, pay their respects, honor him and be rushed away.

Although I do not agree with all they may believe, I can neither disregard nor belittle their devotion. This sacrificial devotion to the man they called the Vicar of Christ (One who stands in His place) accuses me and shames me into facing just how inconsequential I have considered it is to be in the presence of the Living Lord and how I have trivialized fellowship with Him.

There are no pilgrimages. There is no waiting in long lines. We are not expected to rush past and away from Him. He comes to me! He knocks. He waits. He wants me close to Him. He wants to feast with me. And He will be called Emmanuel – *God With Us.*

Lord, forgive me for not hearing and opening the door more readily or acting as if companionship with You did not matter.

 But drops of grief can ne'er repay
The debt of love I owe.
Here Lord, I give myself away
Tis all that I can do.

My Father's Place

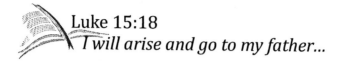
Luke 15:18
I will arise and go to my father...

Here at my father's place I've grown
Tired of familiar things I've known.
I long for a wider open space
So I will leave my father's place.

Tonight from the room where my father sleeps
Come soft sobbing sounds. I know he weeps.
I cannot look on his grieving face
And so I hurry from my father's place.

I have the portion that falls to me
I'm on my own! At last I'm free
Free to run in a different race.
Free at last from my father's place

Here in the far country, what amazing sights!
Reckless days and carefree nights.
My new friends move at a different pace
From what I knew at my father's place.

Hungry, hurting, helpless - alone
No one cares. My money's gone.
Yet there's a memory I can't erase
Of better days at my father's place.

I'll face him confessing all my shame.
No longer worthy to bear his name.
Too great the loss, sin, and disgrace.
"Make me a servant" at my father's place.

There's singing and dancing on my behalf.
Robe - ring - shoes - and a fatted calf.
Tears of joy and a warm embrace.
At last I'm home at my father's place.

 *Lord, thank You for Your gracious welcome when
a sinner returns to You.*

 *I've wandered far away from God
Now I'm coming home.
Too long the path of sin I've trod
Now I'm coming home.*

New Shoes and New Hearts

Ephesians 1:7
*In Him we have redemption through His blood,
the forgiveness of sins, according to the riches
of His grace, which He made to abound toward
us...*

Philippians 4:19
*And my God shall supply all your need
according to His riches in glory by Christ Jesus.*

One day he was in the shoe department at Sears with three excited children who were wearing shabby worn out shoes. After selections were made, the clerk made a phone call and then turned to him and said, "I'm sorry but your payments are past due and we cannot charge this purchase." He left with three disappointed children and an embarrassed wife. He was overcome with humiliation and shame. He was ashamed of the way he had mismanaged his finances. He regretted what he had spent on items of lesser importance. He was hurting for his hurting family.

On another day, he was shamed by a mismanaged life and the waste of God's richest blessings. He was embarrassed by the shabbiness of his soul. He needed more than new shoes. He needed a new heart. He needed mercy. He needed grace.

How could he ask for a new beginning when he had wasted others in the past? Was there any mercy left? Could there still be more grace? When there was no-where else to turn, he turned to the Savior and found Him waiting to forgive him and lavish His grace upon him.

 Lord, what a humiliating thing it is to come to You with nothing to offer You but my shame, my regret and my great need for Your mercy and grace.

Still, I turn to You and find it to be a glorious thing to stand in Your presence and discover the boundless mercy and the amazing grace You are waiting to lavish on me.

 Depth of mercy, can there be
Mercy still reserved for me?
Can my God His wrath forbear
And the chief of sinners spare?

Salvation and Shelling Peas

John 13:35
By this shall all men know that ye are my disciples, if ye have love one to another.

You must understand that my vocabulary was really quite limited and much of it was shaped by expressions I heard in our rural Baptist Church.

One afternoon a number of us were at Taylor Cross' house when Mrs. Cross brought in a few bushels of peas and some pans and asked us to help shell the peas. Carlton Hull was a little older than the rest of us and his pan was filling up more quickly than those of the rest of us. Mrs. Cross stated, "I can tell that Carlton has had experience." With my limited knowledge, the only time I remembered hearing the word "experience" was in reference to the experience of salvation. Sometimes someone would say, "He had the experience." This puzzled me and I kept watching him to see what was so different about his pea shelling and what did being saved have to do with how someone shelled peas?

In later years, I learned that a Christian may or may not shell peas better than anyone else. This was not the measure. Jesus said, "By this shall all men know that you are my disciples if you love one another."

In a competitive world, men struggle to develop certain skills and talents in hopes that these abilities will prove that they are persons of value. One can work at becoming the best athlete, the best tap dancer, the best tambourine player or the best wild bull rider and still miss the assurance of his worth. This is found in receiving the love that the Savior lavishes on us and then by joyfully sharing that love with others.

 Lord, forgive me for the futile struggle to prove my worth in ways that have ignored Your love for me.

 Of His love I shall ever sing
Til above I behold the King
Through eternity my glad song shall be
Of the Savior's redeeming love

Tangled Branches of the Family Tree

Ephesians 2:19
Now, therefore, you are no longer strangers and foreigners, but fellow citizens with the saints and members of the household of God.

Some time ago, a young man married the younger of the Pender sisters. Interestingly enough, some time later his father married the older Pender sister. This caused me to wonder just how the various relationships within the family could be defined.

Since he and his father were married to sisters, his father was now his brother in law. Does he call him dad, brother, or brother/dad?

Since his sister in law is now his step mother, does he call her, sister, mom, or sister/mom?

Since his wife was now his father's sister in law, she was now also his aunt. Hopefully he found a more affectionate name to call her than aunt/wife.

Since he is now his father's brother, he has become his own uncle. Does he call himself uncle/me?

Uncertainty about our relationships is not all that uncommon. We are not always certain as to what we are to expect from others or what they expect of us. So we stumble around, testing the limits of our relationships or fearfully withdrawing into isolation.

Jesus clarified our relationship with God by telling us to call Him our Father. He clarified our relationships with Him by calling us friends for whom He would die. He clarified our relationships with each other by commanding us to love one another with a sacrificial love.

Lord, thank You for calling me to belong to You and for making Your love for me so plain at the cross. Teach me to love those people you have placed in my life.

Blest be the tie that binds
Our hearts in Christian love.
The fellowship of kindred minds
Is like to that above.

Painful Questions

John 21:17
Peter was grieved because He said to him the third time, "Do you love Me?"

Hebrews 4:12
For the word of God is living and powerful, and sharper than any two- edged sword, piercing even to the division of soul and spirit, and of joints and marrow, and is a discerner of the thoughts and intents of the heart.

I have not grieved much because I find it much easier to get lost in the celebration of a cheap and easy sentiment than it is to be pierced by that two edged sword that lays bare my heart. I have longed for and struggled for the approval of others, hoping their endorsement will validate my pretense that I am a loyal follower of the Savior.

Then His Word lays my heart bare and open to the eyes of Him to Whom we must give account.

I am called upon to confess my love for Him, but first, I must acknowledge that it is shamefully less than with all my heart and soul...

Lord, the nails and the sword so clearly reveal Your love for me. As Your Word reveals the thoughts and intents of my heart, forgive the scarcity of evidence of my love for You.

 More love to Thee O Christ
More love to Thee.

See My Hands

John 20: 27-28
Then He said to Thomas, "Reach your finger here, and look at My hands; and reach your hand here, and put it into My side. Do not be unbelieving, but believing." And Thomas answered and said to Him, "My Lord and my God."

I long for a greater faith. For if my faith were greater, I would not be swamped with uncertainties and deluged with doubts and questions of my value. Perhaps, if I were nobler, I would be nearer to God. Maybe if I had been more faithful, I would have a greater faith. While I am wrestling with these concerns, the crucified Savior stands before me, showing me His sword pierced side and His nail scarred hands

Facing these stark testimonies of His endless sacrificial love, my faithlessness flees and I am overwhelmed with the certainty of His forgiving grace and I know that I am His. Yes! I am His forever. Now my feeble faith cries out with Thomas, *My Lord and my God.*

Lord, I cannot make my faith stronger. I can only give to You my doubts and uncertainties as I place my "small as a mustard seed" faith in Your nail scarred hands.

Are you walking alone through the shadows dim?
Place your hand in the nail-scarred hand;
Christ will comfort your heart, put your trust in Him.
Place your hand in the nail-scarred hand.

Place your hand in the nail-scarred hand,
Place your hand in the nail-scarred hand;
He will keep to the end. He's your dearest friend,
Place your hand in the nail-scarred hand.

125

She Doesn't Love Me Anymore

Jeremiah 31:3
Yes, I have loved you with an everlasting love.

There was a day in October of 1941 when I received a brief respite from my struggle against insignificance. During morning recess, Sue told me that Ruth liked me. Suddenly, this fourth grader felt as if he were nine feet tall. I spent the recess hour walking around the school grounds contemplating my new state in life. I was somebody special to somebody special! What more could a person want? I spent the noon hour walking around the school grounds planning a proper, sophisticated response. During afternoon recess I saw her jumping rope out near the swings. I walked over and stood directly in front of her. She kept jumping rope. I gave her a big grin. She continued jumping rope. Finally I called out, "Somebody says you like me." She continued jumping that rope and without missing a beat replied, "I did, but I don't anymore."

Somewhere a young woman is on a bus returning to her parents because someone "doesn't love her any more". A young man sits alone finding it impossible to concentrate on his studies because someone "doesn't love him any more." A child tries to understand why his parents are separating. He does not know why they don't love each other anymore.

In a world of temporary relationships and painful changes, tears are wiped away by a loving God Who declares, "I have loved you with an everlasting love."

The cross tells us how much He has loved us. The good news is that He still does.

Lord, thank You for loving me with a measureless everlasting love.

Every human tie may perish.
Friend to friend unfaithful prove
Mothers cease their own to cherish.
Heaven and earth at last remove.
But no changes can attend Jehovah's love.
But no changes can attend Jehovah's love.

Yard Sale

Proverbs 21:20
*Valuables are safe in a wise person's home;
fools put it all out for yard sales.* (MSG)

1 Thessalonians 5:21
Hold on to what is good. (NLT)

A wise man once said, *"Never sacrifice the permanent on the altar of the immediate."*

You see a yard sale sign and decide you might find a few good bargains. You pass by the used clothing, kitchen and household items and notice a table with a sign saying "special sacrificial bargains." On the table you see the keys to the car, the deed to the house and wedding bands. You ask if these are really for sale and the owner states that you may purchase them. He says, "I don't need the car today and I don't worry about tomorrow so you can have the car for thirty dollars. You can have the deed to the house for forty dollars because the weather is fine today so I'll just stay outside." "I'll give you a good deal on the wedding bands because honoring the vows we once made is quite difficult and they don't mean as much as the once did. There's my daughter, I would trade her for alcohol, drugs, or other cheap thrills. They always temporarily make me feel so good."

How sad it is that often, the most precious and lasting things in life can be traded for the cheap and temporary.

 Lord, please open my eyes to the wonder of Your greatest gifts. Teach me to celebrate and treasure that which really matters. Lead me to surrender them to You that they may be mine to treasure forever.

 All to Jesus I surrender
All to Him I freely give.

Skateboards and Sisters

Hebrews 1:10-12
*"You, Lord, in the beginning laid the foundation
of the earth, and the heavens are the work of
Your hands. They will perish, but You remain;
And they will all grow old like a garment. Like
a cloak You will fold them up, and they will be
changed. But You are the same, and Your years
will not fail."*

Psalm 136:1
*Oh, give thanks to the Lord, for He is good! For
His mercy endures forever.*

Each year in our chapel service on the Wednesday night
before Thanksgiving Day, each person would stand and
complete the following sentence: "I'm thankful for...."
When it came to his turn, one young boy stood and solemnly stated, "I'm thankful for my skateboard and my
sister."

I knew the history behind this statement. He and his
sister had been shifted from one relative to another
and then from one foster home to another. With each
painful move, his sister was with him and he was allowed to keep his skateboard. In a world of change, he
gave thanks for that which remained the same.

Lord, when I am battered by the stormy winds of change, I will praise You for Your goodness that remains the same and for Your steadfast love that endures forever.

 His oath, His covenant, His blood
support me in the whelming flood.
When all around my soul gives way,
He then is all my hope and stay.

Simple Truth

1 Corinthians 15:3
*Christ died for our sins according to the
scriptures.*

The loneliness, pain and sorrow of our Savior on the cross is really beyond my grasp.

The ridicule, the hate and the violence are so far outside my experience that I could never claim that I fully comprehend the event at Calvary. Somehow, I never see the picture quite clearly enough to assert that I have the last word on such matters. I can only praise Him for what I do understand and leave all my questions in the Father's hand because it was His plan.

*Lord, when I would complicate the matters with
questions that I cannot answer and problems
that I cannot solve, remind me of this one simple
truth: You love me.*

Jesus loves me. This I know

Stables And Hearts

John 14:23
Jesus answered and said to him, "If anyone loves Me, he will keep My word; and My Father will love him, and We will come to him and make Our home with him."

At Christmastime, we are moved with pictures of a stable and a manger. Our hearts are touched with reminders of such unimaginable condescension when the Savior stepped down from the glories of Heaven to be born in a stable. Stables look nice when pictured on Christmas cards, but in reality, they are usually cold, uncomfortable, dark, foul smelling and sometimes chaotic. Still, the Savior came to such a place.

One would think that this might be considered the ultimate in humiliation. But wait, He goes further. Later, He said that He and the Father would make Their home with you and with me. Why would He choose to dwell in a heart that is often cold, dark, chaotic and a generally unpleasant place?

There is only one simple but awesome explanation. *My Father will love him.*

Lord, the manger touches my heart. The cross opens my eyes to a love and grace greater than all my sin. Your willingness to live with me staggers my imagination. Change my heart and make it a fit dwelling place for You.

 Love Divine, all loves excelling
Joy of heaven to earth come down
Fix in us Thy humble dwelling;
All Thy faithful mercies crown!
Jesus thou art all compassion,
Pure, unbounded love thou art;
Visit us with thy salvation;
Enter every trembling heart.

State Fair Friendship

2 Peter 1:1
To those who have obtained like precious faith with us by the righteousness of our God and Savior Jesus Christ.

It was a hot afternoon at the state fair in 1968. At a lemonade stand, I met a man who asked me where I was from. When I told him I was from Monroe, he said he was too. We spent a few minutes asking about different people we knew. Over the next several years, I would see him occasionally at a civic club meeting or chance meeting at the mall. Each time we met, he would always ask, "Have you been to the state fair lately?" I'm sure he never lay awake at night wondering how often I attended the fair. Still, I could understand the question because that chance meeting in 1968 was the only thing we knew we had in common.

Twenty five years after that chance meeting, I was the interim pastor at his church. We shared Wednesday night suppers together, wept and prayed together about a troubling matter and on Sundays we celebrated God's amazing grace.

Since then, the state fair has not been mentioned because we have a much greater bond.

Lord, thank You for people you brought into my life. Teach me to remember and celebrate the precious bond we have in You.

 Blest be the tie that binds
Our hearts in Christian love.

Taking Care Of God

Matthew 25:40
*And the King will answer and say to them,
"Assuredly, I say to you, inasmuch as you did it
to one of the least of these, My brethren, you
did it to Me."*

Our church is blessed with great leadership. The pastor's brilliant sermons make God's word so plain and clear. The choir members, soloists, instrumentalists and other musical groups lift our hearts with such beautiful soul stirring music. Staff members give outstanding and effective leadership in the many areas of the life of the church. Life Groups (We used to call them Sunday School Classes) are blessed with great Bible teachers. Deacons and committee members give our church wise counsel regarding plans and decisions to be made.

Then there are those who may be considered of lesser importance. You don't see them on the platform. You don't hear them speaking or singing. They are in another area of the church taking care of the little ones.

Ask a man who spent Sunday morning in the children's department and he might reply, "I took care of God. When He was hungry, I gave Him a cookie. When He was thirsty, I gave Him some juice. I made one of the children stop biting Him. I told Him a story and sang a song with Him. When He wet his pants, I changed Him into dry clothing. When He cried, I held Him and rocked Him."

This claim may seem to be rather outlandish, but Jesus told of the time when the King would say to those on His right hand, *"In as much as you did it unto one of the least of these, My brothers, you did it unto Me."*

Lord, teach me to accept any assignment You may give me with joy and gratitude. Remind me that any task You may give me is a holy privilege. Teach me to celebrate the honor of service. Lead me to handle my task in such a way that one day I may hear You say, "Well Done!"

Jesus loves the little children.
All the children of the world.

Temporary Gifts

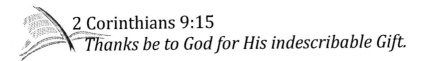

2 Corinthians 9:15
Thanks be to God for His indescribable Gift.

When Leroy was informed that he had received a gift of twenty dollars, he said, "I think I'll buy Mrs. Rimes a Christmas present because she is the best housemother on the campus and she's the nicest woman in the whole world."

He persistently asked for someone to take him shopping. During the Thanksgiving holidays, one of the staff members took him to the mall and he bought a large bottle of ladies cologne. She then helped him wrap it.

On the day after Thanksgiving, Mr. Rimes and the boys put up the Christmas tree but before they were finished, Leroy brought his gift, placed it under the tree and proudly announced, "This is for Mrs. Rimes and nobody better touch it."

During the following week, when Mrs. Rimes refused to let him go outside until he completed his homework, he stormed into the den, grabbed the present, took it to his room and threw it under the bed. The following day, he returned it to the tree. A few days later, when Mrs. Rimes insisted that he clean his room before going out to wait for the bus, he told her he hated her and hoped she died before he got home from school. Again he grabbed the present from under the tree and threw it under his bed. The following evening it was returned to its place beneath the tree.

Again, when Mrs. Rimes did not settle an argument with some other boys to his satisfaction, (You guessed it!) the present was taken back again. On the day of the Christmas party, he handed the package with the frayed wrapping to her and wished her a Merry Christmas.

Too often our giving is based upon the circumstances of the moment or our changeable, unpredictable feelings.

God's gift was also based on our circumstances and His feelings. The circumstance was that sinners like us need a Savior. The feeling was an unchanging sacrificial love.

These have never changed.

Lord forgive me for my shifting, changing love for You. Thank You for loving me with a love that has not changed.

I love Thee because Thou hast first loved me,
And purchased my pardon on Calvary's tree;
I love Thee for wearing the thorns on Thy brow;
If ever I loved Thee, my Jesus, 'tis now.

The Beauty of Holiness

Psalm 29:2
Give unto the Lord the glory due to His name;
Worship the Lord in the beauty of holiness.

I never thought much about the term, "beauty of holiness," until recently when I was thinking of weddings.

On one occasion, just before the wedding ceremony was to begin I overheard the bride make a very cutting remark to her mother. Then, she was obviously displeased with her father as he escorted her down the aisle. When the groom was to walk with her up the steps to the platform, he made the unforgivable mistake of taking her hand instead of her elbow. She glared at him with a look that seemed to say, "you can't do anything right."

I briefly considered suggesting that we call the whole thing off. The flowers and the elegant bridal gown did little to make the occasion a beautiful event.

Fortunately, other weddings have not been like this. I am deeply moved by the beauty of two people who love each other so much that they joyfully commit themselves totally and permanently to each other.

When one considers the limitless love displayed at the cross and responds daily with a total commitment of himself to the crucified Savior, that is holiness. That is beauty.

 Lord, please lead me to commit myself to You each day. May my love for You be a clear reflection of Your sacrificial love for me.

 This is my earnest plea;
More love O Christ to Thee
More love to Thee.
More love to Thee.

The Chauffeur

2 Corinthians 5:21
For He made Him Who knew no sin to be sin for us, that we might become the righteousness of God in Him.

Because he could neither read nor write, John found it impossible to find a job until one day, the employment office called him and asked if he could drive and John assured them that he could. They informed him that Professor Jones was the smartest man in the world and would be lecturing in cities across the country. Since Professor Jones was afraid of flying, he needed a driver. John was provided a chauffeur's uniform and began driving the smartest man in the world from one town to another where auditoriums were packed with people wanting to hear the brilliant lecturer.

Every night, crowds came to large lecture halls and auditoriums to hear Professor Jones' magnificent lecture. John was there, basking in the adoration given his boss. John listened intently but never understood what the lecture was about. One evening after a few months of traveling, they were in the hotel getting ready to go to the lecture hall when Professor Jones confided that he did not feel well and wished he did not have to give his lecture. John replied, "I can give it for you. I've heard that speech so many times I have it memorized and can give it word for word." The men then exchanged clothing. Professor Jones dressed himself in the chauffeur's uniform and John wore the Brooks Brothers suit. As they entered the hall, Professor Jones carried the briefcase for John. When it was time, John came to the platform and gave a flawless repetition of the lecture he had heard so many times before. At the end of the speech, the crowd stood, applauded and cheered, indicating that they were honored to be in the presence of one with such intelligence and understanding.

When the applause was finally over, one of the attendees stood and stated that he had a question. He asked, "If your hypothesis is valid, if ten tons of ozone were released over the North Pole at a height of thirty thousand feet, what would be the eventual change of the temperature in Argentina?"

John stood there for a long time without speaking. Finally the questioner asked, "Is the question too hard for you?" John replied, "No, in fact, the question is such a simple and easy one, I'll let my chauffeur answer it for me."

I suppose it's a natural thing to want to appear stronger or brighter than we really are. We would also prefer to appear to be cleaner and more righteous than we really are. However, sooner or later, we face those matters for which we have no answers and must turn to the One Who came to trade places with us.

Lord, the fact that You would exchange Your glory for my shame is beyond my comprehension. Still, I bow in Your presence and thank You for taking my place.

 Bearing shame and scoffing rude,
In my place, condemned He stood
Sealed my pardon with His blood
Hallelujah, what a Savior.

Tennis Balls

2 Chronicles 6:29
...when each one knows his own burden and his own grief, and spreads out his hands to this temple.

After recovering from surgery, I needed to put some tennis balls on the legs of my walker so it would slide more smoothly across the floor.

I went to the sporting goods store and parked in the handicapped parking space. I decided to try to walk into the store without my walker. Walking was still very painful so my walk into the store was slow, painful and with a very obvious limp. By the time I got into the store, I needed to lean on the counter for just a little while to get some relief. When the young lady behind the counter asked what she could do for me, I told her I needed some tennis balls. I think she tried to hide her flabbergasted state, but still, she gave me an astonished "you've got to be kidding" expression.

When she regained her composure she asked me, "Clay court or hard court?" My telling her, "whichever is cheapest" did little to relieve her discomfort. I decided not to tell her what they were for. As I was leaving, I saw her reflection in the storefront window. She was shaking her head as if wondering if anyone knew that this old guy was out and making important decisions on his own. She never knew that I was aware of my athletic limitations and my need for help with my pain.

Pain and grief are personal. The invitation to talk with the Lord about them is also personal.

 Lord, others do not always know or understand my hurt or my need. Thank You for knowing, understanding and caring.

 O yes He cares, I know He cares.
His heart is touched with my grief.

What If We Had a Wreck and Had to Go to the Hospital?

Psalm 136:1
Give thanks to the Lord, for He is good!
His faithful love endures forever. (NLT)

As boys, when we would try to avoid the bath and get by with a surface appearance of cleanliness, Mama would exclaim, "What if we had a wreck and had to go to the hospital!"

We heard it so often that we concluded if we ever had a wreck and we all ended up in the hospital, I am sure that she would have been concerned about broken bones, lacerations and other injuries, but she would also be overcome with anxiety, fearful that under the bright lights in an examination room, folks would discover that Mrs. Powell's boys were not as clean as they had appeared to be.

One element of a crisis is that, in addition to what it may do to us, is the fear of what it may reveal about us. The exam at school may reveal that we are not as knowledgeable as we thought we were. The job evaluation may reveal that we are not as competent as we needed to be. The audit may reveal that our finances are not in the order they should be. The medical exam may reveal that we are not as healthy as we need to be.

When these fearsome matters are placed in the hands of God, we may also learn what it reveals about Him. He is sovereign and He is good. He can take this disaster and use it to accomplish His ultimate loving purpose in our lives.

Under the bright light on the Damascus road, Paul discovered that he was not as righteous as he had thought he was, but this *chief of sinners* also discovered the forgiving grace of God.

 Lord, when predicaments come that strip me of my superficial image and rob me of my false hopes, remind me that I am Yours, that You are good and Your steadfast love endures forever.

 Blessed Jesus, Blessed Jesus,
   Thou Hast loved us, love us still.

Who Dresses You

Galatians 3:27
For as many of you as were baptized into Christ have put on Christ.

My friend, Earl Mercer, once told me of an accident that occurred one night just outside Winnfield, Louisiana.

When the Deputy Sheriff was writing his report, he asked the elderly gentleman who drove the pickup, "Sir, did you have your dimmers on?" He replied, "I just wear what the missus lays out for me."

There are those who lay out our garments for us. Some would lay out a clown suit suggesting that you are not to be taken seriously. Others may lay out prison stripes advertising your mistakes of the past. Others may lay out a diaper suggesting that you lack the maturity to handle life's difficulties.

There are times we can choose what to wear as we heed Paul's instruction to *"Put on the whole armor of God."* Ultimately, we let the Savior dress us and then we can proclaim: *I will greatly rejoice in the Lord, My soul shall be joyful in my God; For He has clothed me with the garments of salvation, He has covered me with the robe of righteousness, As a bridegroom decks himself with ornaments, And as a bride adorns herself with her jewels.* (Isaiah 61:10)

Lord, what an awesome thing it is to consider that you would exchange Your glory for my shame.

 Dressed in His righteousness alone
Faultless to stand before the throne.

Walk In the Light

 1 John 1:7
But if we walk in the light as He is in the light, we have fellowship with one another, and the blood of Jesus Christ His Son cleanses us from all sin.

If I walk in the light I will face exposure and vulnerability. In the light there are no secrets, no hidden agendas, no concealed animosity, no jealousy nor other hidden destructive attitudes. The light reveals who I am and what I am.

And yet, it is in the light that we have true fellowship. This blessed fellowship is based on truth and reality. Here, in the light, I do not have to wonder if I would be loved and accepted if someone really knew me.

As I step into the light through confession there is forgiveness, cleansing, and fellowship.

Lord, forgive my tendency to linger in the darkness, lest I be seen as I am. Thank You for inviting me into the light that I may be forgiven and made clean.

How beautiful to walk in the steps of the Savior
Stepping in the light. Stepping in the light.
How beautiful to walk in the steps of the Savior
Led in paths of light.

The School Teacher's Wife *

Hosea 2:19
And I will betroth thee unto me forever; yea, I will betroth thee unto me in righteousness, and in judgment, and in loving kindness, and in mercies.

Mary was attractive, pleasant, and likable. Mary could not read. Her parents could not read and the father reminded them time and again that he could not read and had made it just fine. In spite of her father's claim that reading was absolutely unnecessary, she felt that the inability to read was a sentence to loneliness and isolation. She had never smiled at the surprise ending of an O'Henry story, never laughed at limericks of Ogden Nash nor ever been touched by the beauty of the poetry of Elizabeth Barrett Browning. When she went into the local stores, folks grinned at one another and talked of how strange that she could not read but someone would point out that her family didn't read. Once she tried to go inside the school building but was told, *"You can't come in here because this a school and you can't read."* So she spent her days in isolation wondering what it would be like in the stores if folks smiled at her rather than about her. She wondered what it would be like to be in a school where everyone could read and talk of interesting things.

One day the new school teacher came to town. He was drawn to her by her gentle smile and touched by the sadness in her eyes. He liked her and wanted to spend time with her. He walked home with her and stood on the porch and visited for a while. The community was shocked that a teacher would be seen publicly with a member of that family that did not read. They told him, *"She and her folks are not our kind. The"y don't read."* He was warned to stay from such folks but he told them, *"I came not to call the college graduates, but the uneducated to learning."* Word spread throughout the community that the teacher even eats with folks that don't read. In the days that followed, he would go by her house in the evening, sit on the porch and visit with her and her parents. The teacher and Mary took long walks and, day by day, grew closer. One evening as they sat on the porch he declared his love for her and asked her to marry him. With this, Mary began to weep and said that she could never marry a teacher because she could not read. He took her in his arms and told her that all that mattered to him was his love for her and that he would teach her to read. The community was scandalized by the news but still came to the wedding and watched the teacher take the hand of this woman who could not read and publicly claim her as his wife. After this, when Mary walked into the stores she was greeted warmly because, after all, she was the teacher's wife. When she visited the school, students were delighted to see her because she was the teacher's wife. Her greatest delight was not her new standing in the community or the school, but instead it was that time she sat at home with her husband, her teacher, as he taught her to read. In the evenings, if you were to walk by their house you may see her smiling at the unique ending of an O'Henry story. You may hear her laugh out loud at the limericks of Ogden Nash. You may see a tear of joy on her cheek as she reads words like *How do I love you, let me count the ways*. You see such joy in her eyes as she delights in knowing that she is loved by the teacher. That she is the teacher's wife.

More than anything else, Jesus was called *The Teacher*. Just think who we are! The beloved bride of the Teacher. The Scriptures call us *The Bride Of Christ*.

* First published in *Daily Grace* by Clarence Powell